The Revolution of Eve

The Revolution of Eve

C. Alexandra Allen

Library of Congress Number:		2001119673
ISBN #:	Hardcover	1-4010-3977-4
	Softcover	1-4010-3934-0

This is a work of fiction. Names, characters, places and incidents either are the product of the author's imagination or are used fictitiously, and any resemblance to any actual persons, living or dead, events, or locales is entirely coincidental.

This book was printed in the United States of America.

To order additional copies of this book, contact:
Xlibris Corporation
1-888-7-XLIBRIS
www.Xlibris.com
Orders@Xlibris.com

Contents

-ALLE

Mommy & Daddy, I love you each dearly. This book is dedicated to the both of you.

To those who ever doubted that this could be done…it's done.

To myself, all I can do is try.

Acknowledgments

Each of us has touched the life of another person. Some of these experiences are surreal. Nevertheless, regardless of the experience, we grow as members of the human race by tasting the bitter and the sweet.

To the Creator, Mother/Father God-*You know my heart and soul in its purest form. Thank you for your divine inspiration, protection, and guidance. Most of all, thank you for your forgiveness.*

To Maya Angelou, Toni Morrison, Nikki Giovanni, & Langston Hughes-*Thank you for picking up your pens to craft pieces of art that will be enjoyed for generations. You showed me the power of the written word. Whenever I pick up my pen it is in tribute to each of you.*

To All the Brothers I've Loved-*Thanks for the love, the passion, and the pain. You each have taught me about myself. I'm forever grateful.*

To My Soulmate-*Please make yourself seen.*

To Spelman College-*Thanks for teaching me about my "sheroes" and showing me what it truly means to be a Spelman Woman.*

To Everyone Who Has Come Into My Life for A Reason or A Season-*Thanks for touching my soul and my life.*

-ALLE

Foreword

It is a disturbing ideology that the most highly revered poets in the world are not people of color. I am in no way attempting to take away from the literary prowess of poets such as Anne Bradstreet, Robert Frost, Walt Whitman, Sylvia Plath and others. However, I believe that efforts should be made to equally recognize the literary contributions and accomplishments of poets of color. Otherwise, we continue to reinforce the inequities which have divided our nation into four worlds: Black vs. White and The Have's vs. The Have Not's. In each case, the majority group establishes the standards which minority groups must emulate in order to gain mainstream acceptance. As a result, artists who choose to "go against the grain" rarely attain the notoriety that they rightfully deserve.

The title of this work carries a dual meaning. First, I want to present a different image of Eve. She was more than a childbearer and a companion for Adam. As a rebellious female, Eve was a woman who recognized her power as a woman, as a sexual being and as a mother. Secondly, I want to dispel the notion that Eve was a majority female. If we have all been created in the likeness of God, is there a reason why I should not be a reflection of Eve? Could she have had brown eyes and kinky hair? Could she have been an African?

I offer this piece to you as a descendant of the first woman to walk the face of the earth: Eve. This book is an exploration of various life experiences. I hope it sparks conversation, as well as, controversy. I challenge readers to use each verse as a vehicle to discover their own truth.

The Letter

Dear Children,

My little brown ones, we are the beginning. There were none before us, but there will be many after us. My eyes have been opened to the coldness which will exist in this new world. I can see clearly that life will be difficult in the years to come. Soon, you will leave this place to settle in every corner of the world forming a kaleidoscope of color. But, rest assured. Each of you will thrive and survive regardless of the circumstances of your departure and arrival. Just hold your heads up high. Stay strong. Stay focused. Stay grounded. Stay proud. If you must die, die on your feet. Never allow yourself to die on your hands and knees.

I look forward to the day when we will all meet in this place to walk barefoot in fields of Peace and Joy. Then, we'll go purify ourselves in the bosom of the Nile. When that day comes, the cleansing of our minds and the revitalization of our souls will be long overdue.

The Creation of Eve

"And the rib which the Lord God had taken from man, made he a woman, and brought her unto the man. And Adam said, 'This is now bone of my bones, and flesh of my flesh: she shall be called Woman, because she was taken out of Man.' Therefore, shall a man leave his father and his mother, and shall cleave unto his wife: and they shall be one flesh. And they were both naked, the man and his wife, and were not ashamed."

"Now the serpent was more subtle than any beast of the field which the Lord God had made. And he said unto the woman, 'Yea, hath God said, Ye shall not eat of every tree of the Garden?' And the woman said to the serpent, 'We may eat of the fruit of the trees of the garden. But of the fruit of the tree which is in the midst of the garden, God hath said, Ye shall not eat it, neither shall Ye touch it, lest Ye die.' And the serpent said unto the woman, 'Ye shall not surely die. For God doth know that in the day ye eat thereof, then your eyes shall be opened, and ye shall be as gods, knowing good and evil.' And when the woman saw that the tree was good for food, and that it was pleasant to the eyes, and a tree be desired to make one wise, she took of the fruit thereof, and did eat, and gave unto her husband with her. And he did eat."

"And the eyes of them both were opened, and they knew that they were naked. And they sewed fig leaves together, and made aprons. And they heard the voice of the Lord God walking in the garden in the cool of the day: and Adam and his wife hid themselves from the presence of the Lord God amongst the trees of the garden. And the Lord God called unto Adam, and said unto him, 'Where art thou?' And he said, 'I heard thy voice in the garden, and I was afraid, because I was naked. And I hid myself.' And he said, 'Who told thee that thou wast naked? ' Hast thou eaten of the tree, whereof I commanded thee that thou shouldest not eat?"

"And the man said, 'The woman whom thou gavest to be with me, she gave me of the tree, and I did eat.' And the Lord God said unto the woman, 'What is this that thou hast done?' And the woman said, 'The serpent beguiled me, and I did eat.' And the Lord God said unto the serpent, 'Because thou hast done this, thou art cursed above all cattle, and above every beast of the field: upon thy belly shall thou eat all the days of thy life.' And I will put enmity between thee and the woman, and between thy seed and her seed. It shall bruise thy head, and thou shalt bruise his heel."

"Unto the woman he said, 'I will greatly multiply thy sorrow and thy conception. In sorrow thou shalt bring forth children and thy desire shall be to thy husband, and he shall rule over thee.' And unto Adam he said, 'Because thou hast hearkened unto the voice of thy wife, and hast eaten of the tree, cursed is the ground for thy sake. In sorrow shalt thou eat of it all the days of thy life.' Thorns also and thistles shall it bring forth to thee and thou shalt eat the herb of the field. In the sweat of thy face shalt thou eat bread, till thou return unto the ground. For out of it wast thou taken. For dust thou art, and unto dust shalt thou return."

"And Adam called his wife's name Eve because she was the mother of all living. Unto Adam also and to his wife did the Lord God make coats of skins, and clothed them. And the Lord God said,

'Behold the man is become as one of us, to know good and evil: and now, lest he put forth his hand, and take also of the tree of life, and eat, and live forever.' Therefore the Lord God sent him forth from the Garden of Eden, to till the ground from whence he was taken. So he drove out the man; and he placed at the east of the Garden of Eden Cherubim's, and a flaming sword which turned every way, to keep the way of the tree of life. And Adam knew Eve his wife. And she conceived, and bare Cain, and said, I have gotten a man from the Lord."

(Taken from Genesis 2:22 through Genesis 4:1 of The King James Version of the Holy Bible)

GENESIS

-ALLE

Journey

For centuries, I've been searching for you
Only you can fill this undying need
Molded in a likeness
Formed from dust
Took your rib and created me
Connected from the start but we never met

When I became the Queen of Egypt
You carried my crown
Faithful servant, you placed it on my head
Eyes and smile etched in my memory, but an identity concealed

When Miss Ann sent me to the store for flour I caught your eye while walkin' past the field
Masta sho'got ya wurkin' hard pickin' that cotton
With sweat pourin' down your chest you looked at me like we've met before
That familiar smile triggered sweet old memories of way back when
I passed the same field until Freedom Day never to see that smile again

When those White boys ordered me to use the Colored fountain and tried to beat me
You saved me

Pulled me out of the confusion
Who were you?

When I needed protection, your arms shielded me from harm
When I doubted myself, you convinced me that I could do anything
When I was sick, you healed me
You showed me laughter again
My angel, you are always there when I need you
And I know who you are now
You are my GOD

Brown Butta-Fly

I nurtured you for 40 weeks give or take
Gave you everything to make you great
Protected you with myself in a liquid filled cocoon
Words penetrated your mind
Sound permeated your soul giving you rhythm
Love embodied your heart and mine
You are mine
Our link is eternal

Such a precious gift to the world
Eyes like mine
Both innocent and experienced at the same time
Countenance of a young warrior marked in the first hours of his existence
You are Ibo, Cherokee, Jamaican, Yoruba, Iroquois and Haitian
From Africa to America
America to Africa and everything in between
A mosaic of ivory, chestnut, caramel, black cherry, and onyx
With pride, beauty and infinite wisdom
With a history of centuries of resilience, power and might
So, fight
This is all the strength you'll need beloved
Now, pull from the past

Propel yourself through the future
Now, fly
Fly, my little brown butta-fly
Fly

Images Of You

I peered unto the waters to find something that came of no surprise
I was Black
I gazed unto the calm waters and remembered the struggles of my ancestors
I thought
I wrote
Then, I left those waters and walked through pastures whose soil was soaked with blood
It too, was Black

Morning turned night as I sat under a beauteous white blossomed tree swaying in the wind like angels wings fluttering against a starry sky
Her 400 year-old roots were thick and strong
Past and Present deeply embedded themselves in the soil and covered the earth

As I touch myself, I feel the movement of my unborn seed
One day, they will come to the waters and receive inspiration
One night, they will commune with nature on the Creator's land
Reflect
Write
Write about their pride, their dignity
And give thanks that they are such a beautiful, blessed color
BLACK

Mother Time

She never changes.
Here's a second-recognize it.
A minute-cherish it.
An hour-experience it.
A day-live it.
Receive it.
It's a gift given to you.

So, here's another second-take it.
Another minute-feel it.
Another hour-use it wisely.
Another day-enjoy it.
Share it with who you love.
Time holds memories of seconds, minutes, hours and days gone by.
It clears the path for the future and gives more time to make memories.

Time never changes.
You change as the butterfly does.
From captive to free.
Naïve to wise.
Young to old.
Hate to love.
Sad to happy.
Disbelief to belief.

Trust it.
Trust each second, minute, hour, and day held for you.
Nurture it.
Time is constant.
It never changes.
It simply comes to pass.

High

I find myself having visions of purple crescent moons
Distorting my reality like the snow I saw in a 95 degree June
The sun which shined last night
And the sight of falling red rain
As I escape this twisted world once again

A world where disease
Will bring you to your knees
A world where violence spreads like infections
Sometimes your only protection
Is to save your soul

There is a searing pain in my heart
Because I've torn lives apart
Today, guilt burns my body like hot coal
Then, I heard a voice say "it's time to sanctify your soul"
Time to sanctify my soul?
Time to sanctify my soul
Sanctify my soul

With each tear
I erase memories of the years when I did wrong
All in the name of trying to belong
Trying to get along

Suddenly I shed 20 years of pain like dead skin
In an instant
I've been forgiven for all my sins
A new life begins
With a sanctified soul
A sanctified soul
Sanctified soul
Soul

Nameless

It's been 10,220 days since I can to be
Lately, I'm struggling with the person that I see
In the mirror there is a sinner
A saint
A human being who questions what decisions to make
All in fear that I may somehow taint your master plan
What do you want me to do?
Can you tell me who I am?

Should I remain as pure as newly fallen snow?
Or, transform myself into the person that the world should love and know?
I'm standing before you with my heart exposed
Wondering if I should turn left or right
And if the life that I'm leading has been ordained by your sight

Lord, can you tell me who I am?
Who do you want me to be?
I'm your child
Name me

Vertical, Not Horizontal

When you throw an obstacle in my path
Or, try to sway my Black soul in another direction
I'll stand firm on my foundation
Always vertical, never horizontal

When you express your jealousy by slashing me with razor tongues
I'll never lose sight of my goals
I'll continue to be vertical, never horizontal

Do you expect a sista to give up?
No, I'll never be out of the race of life
The Creator saw to it that I had the might to endure
Struggle
Strife

My ancestors were Queens and Kings
Therefore, I can do all things
'Cuz I was created to be vertical, not horizontal

ALLE

I Am A Woman

I am a woman.
Let me rephrase.
I am an electrifying woman.
I bare souls with my deep brown eyes.
I make men break into a sweat with my voluptuous hips, and silky smooth thighs.
The sultry voice that I possess caresses the ear of my listener
Like one would sensually touch the body of a lover in a moment of passion.

I am a powerful woman.
Powerful enough to move snow-capped mountains with my determination.
I am an intelligent woman who soars above the clouds on wings of knowledge.
I am a caring woman who embraces her brothers and sisters in arms of understanding.
The love in my heart is great enough to engulf the earth, sky, sea and beyond.

Like the sun, I warm the earth with my inner spirit.
I am special.
So special, that the moon shines in my favor every night.

I am a woman who fights wars without weapons.
I fight the aggressor with words.
Still, I reign victorious.
How many people can do that?

Standing firmly on the foundation that has been laid for me,
I vow to love myself and those surrounding me eternally.

I am a Black woman

Warrior

He carries the world on his shoulders
While the sun beams on his back
Browning him
Crowning him
Yet, he stands erect without a bead of sweat
While others would holler fuck this world
And buckle under the pressure
His legs never tremble from the weight
Somehow he carries on
He is a warrior
The man who bears wounds that don't bleed
The one who can't be knocked to his knees
Though you may try
Try to deny him of everything which is rightfully his

Then, you throw his weaker brothers into a man made business nonetheless
A new gig called the prison industrial complex
Yet, he stands erect
Never dropping a bead of sweat
In hope that one day his people will be elevated
And his brother can one day become strong enough to help him carry the world

IT'S A COLD, COLD WORLD

Why?

Sometimes people become inspired to do things for others
Why not?
Aren't we all sisters and brothers
I watch out for you
You do the same for me
Isn't that the way it's supposed to be?
Livin' large in the land of the free
Is that why there's so much homelessness and poverty?

There were those who rose above oppression to make freedom ring
So why do we spare the lives of murders and kill a man like King?

Are We Free?

Are we free?
This is the question.
Our necks may be lighter because we no longer have metal wrapped around them
And our arms and legs can move a little better because the shackles have been removed
But, are we really free?
What about our men-tal-it-y?

While freedom brings elation,
Look at these situations and
Spark some conversations about what it means to be free

Scene 1:
I replaced my chains with a designer suit made by a man who said that his clothes weren't designed for people of color
Forget "for us by us" made by our brothers
But, his gear is so tight
I had to buy enough to make that bigots bankroll right

Scene 2:
I've penetrated the highest leadership positions in corporate America
Yet, if you let your subscription to BE lapse you may not recognize that I'm the HNIC

I just shortened my name for more global acceptance you see
Are we free?

Scene 3:
I allow my own brothers to put me back on the auction block
I'm some 36-24-36 fine stock
It's just that the money they're paying me for this music video is so good
I don't mind shaking my naked ass to the beat and simulating sex acts on a car hood
While some dude brags about what he can do to me while in mount
With millions in his mouth and only a few G's in his bank account
Are we really free?

Scene 4:
I stand on a dark street corner every night
Gettin' nervous whenever I see carlights
Cuz I don't know if it's a customer or a rival
My grandma always taught me that this life was wrong
But, after I got shot my football scholarship was gone
So, here I am fightin' for survival on these streets
Shit
A nigga gotta eat

Scene 5:
I consider myself one of the righteous
I'm a prophet
I'm the one who got turned around spiritually in the pen
Then, I got turned out
I'm gay only for the stay
And yet I write home everyday
To tell my lady how much I love her and my child
Like the Creator hasn't heard my lies from far away
Are we really free?

Are we really free?
Or, are we modern day slaves?
Remember.
You have to have to be free in mind to truly be free

41 Times (R.I.P. Diallo)

41 times
They shot at him 41 times
They shot at him 41 times
Everytime I turn on the news I see his body in a chalk outline
They shot at him 41 times
Click. (1x)
Click. (2x)
Click. (3x)
Click. (4x)
Click. (5x)
Click. (6x)
Click. (7x)
Click. (8x)
Click. (9x)
Click. (10x)

How many bullets can a body hold?
How many shots do you have to fire to make a body cold?
41 Times?
Click. (11x)
Click. (12x)
Click. (13x)
Click. (14x)
Click. (15x)

Click. (16x)
Click. (17x)
Click. (18x)
Click. (19x)
Click. (20x)

41 times?

That's equal to one bullet for each time you abused your authority in the last hour
All done in the name of power
As you hide behind the badge with a license to kill
Anybody. Anytime. Anyplace.
In the name of protecting and serving
As each of you squeeze the trigger until chambers empty
And never pull back
Where is the honor in that?
Who else will you shoot at 41 Times?

Click. (21x)
Click. (22x)
Click. (23x)
Click. (24x)
Click. (25x)
Click. (26x)
Click. (27x)
Click. (28x)
Click. (29x)
Click. (30x)

41 Times.

Click. (31x)
Click. (32x)
Click. (33x)

Click. (34x)
Click. (35x)
Click. (36x)
Click. (37x)
Click. (38x)
Click. (39x)
Click. (40x)
Click (41x)

41 Times.
They shot at him 41 times.

Video Star

Whenever I turn on my T.V
I see your half-naked ass blasted all over BET
Bouncin' and jigglin' to the beat like you've been told
How many dollars does it take for you to sell your soul?

See the camera should not be filming your coochie
Those takes are reserved for porn stars and hoochies
You should demand to be captured for the beauty that you are
And not allow yourself to be straddled and stretched across an expensive car
'Cause at the end of the day no one even knows who your are
For fans remember the work of the artist not the video star

Untitled II

From the back of the bus
To the back of a limousine
The child with a 4.0
The child with hoop dreams

From Colored
To Negro
To African-American
To "People of Color"
Too Black
Not Black enough

From coach class
To middle class
Upper class
No class
From mamies and menstrual shows
To tokenism
The realism…
Racism
From the cotton fields
To corporate seats
From million dollar mansions
To living on the streets

Things Done Changed

Take me back to when curls were "care free"
Michael Jackson was brown like me
And Kid-N-Play was "Gettin' Funky"
Back when we fought with our hands
And battles took place between crews on dance floors
Back when I caught the Q4
And danced to "It Takes Two" until my feet got sore
Back when we sported Fendi and MCM suits and boots
And the karat was 14
As we rocked 2, 3, or 4 finger rings

Back when Run-DMC had us walk this way
And you could see LL Cool J on the Ave on any day
While Pete Rock & CL Smooth reminisced over you
Back when Roxanne got her revenge
And Salt-N-Pepa got us to push it
While leather African medallions swung around our necks
And we bent down to clean our new white kicks with toothbrushes

Back when I went to Sunrise Cinemas for a movie
Then, walked over to the mall to catch the dollar van
Back when I slow danced to "I Need Love" at the house party
And healed a broken heart over "All Cried Out Over You"

Back when we pumped Special Ed's "I Got It Made" in a fully loaded Jetta
And ladies sweated Big Daddy Kane's beautiful complexion before light became right

Back when high top fades and gumbi's were the cut of choice
And people were trippin' off of Michel'le's voice
Back when we were "Krush Groovin" body movin'
And Shabba-Doo was in Electric Boogaloo

Back when your hat was a Kangol
Leather like Kool Moe Dee's
Or, raccoon
And your glasses were called "gazelles" trimmed in gold or diamonds to match your teeth
Back when New York Hot Tracks would play the flyest videos
Donny Simpson had Video Soul
And Bentley's was always live on Saturday nights

Back in the days of double-dutch contests
Playin' spin the bottle and 7-Up
With jellies and Chinese shoes on our feet we played dodgeball in the street
Back when a young boy kicked it to a girl on a piece of loose-leaf
"Do you like me?" . . . it said
"Will you go with me?"...it said
Then, we checked the box "Yes" or "No" and sent it back
As our friends smiled and laughed
Back when you were chillin'
And clockin' cuties
And everything was F-R-E-S-H

Back when life was free
And young people lived longer than age 23
Back when life was fun
Like it should be

Blue Eyes

I saw her on 125th street in front of the Apollo
Standing next to a brother with an afro
Symmetrically round
Surrounded by folk from BK to the Boogie Down
He chanted "Are you down with Brown?"
I mean this brother was dashiki down
Pumping his right hand in the air shouting "REV-OL-UTION"
As a White woman pushed through the crowd to stand by his side

She looked so proud
Her statuesque body
Enveloped in blue-black skin
With a caesar cut so close that I could see the mink oil glistening on her scalp
So, natural
So, beautiful

Walking with the grace of an Alvin Ailey dancer
Strides as swift as a gazelle
Knowing herself well
Radiating confidence with each movement
Clearing paths
Every man on the street wanted her math

So, I ran to catch up with this sister
She smiled and said "Hi"
Then, in all her natural essence
She batted her baby blue eyes

She

Her once brown back
Is now a blackish-blue hue
All hand-crafted by a man she loves
A man she once knew

Her MAC makeup camouflages the bruises on her forehead
On her eyelids
On her cheeks
While Versace clothes cover the physical scars of previous weeks

Each night
She prays for a day
When she'll no longer be greeted by swinging fists
Instead of hugs
The day when she'll no longer desire to slash her own wrists
As fresh blood stains settle in bedroom rugs

Still, she says "he's gonna change"
"It's just some things in his life that he has to re-arrange"
Yet, in the past 11 years
She's shed nothing but her dignity and tears
And she clings to him still
Not recognizing that this kind of love can kill

Set It Off

Could it be?
136 years since emancipation and still not free
Got me showin' ID's
With all these hidden cameras beamin' down on me
Invadin' all my privacy
While neighborhood hustlers sell crack on street corners
Pimps sell our mothers, daughters and sisters by the act
By the hour
Self-professed ghetto-preneurs schoolin' our children on the power of the almighty dollar
When I get out there everyday
Makin' my contribution to society in a positive way
As young brothers and sisters carry guns instead of school books
Talkin' about killin' each other
Instead of talkin' about revolution
Callin' themselves niggers
Itchy fingers on triggers
Creatin' business for grave diggers
By playin' Russian Roulette and other games of hit and miss
What kinda shit is this?

Last week, I heard a twelve year- old sayin' that she was tryin' to get pregnant
Tryin' to bring another life into the world

Thinking it'll make her a woman, but still a little girl
Man, the concept of this is wild
You just got out of Pampers
Now, you want taxpayers to buy them for your child?
While your 18 year-old boy/friend cruises around town
Tellin' all his boys how you get down
Callin' you loose
Loose as a size 24 dress on an anorexic body
And dirty like an untreated sewer
But, he loves you right?

Then, I saw these two brothers on TV re-cent-ly
Called themselves "Gospel Gangsters"
Said they were keepin' it real for Jesus and the streets you see
Sounds a bit confusing to me
'Cause you can't serve the Creator and the streets too
Bible in the left hand
While the right hand holds a Glock
Brothers you need to check the clock
The time is now
You can only serve one master
Not two
I thought you knew

But, again I digress
Got some more stuff to get off my chest
What's up with these millennium paper bag tests?
Sense-less
What will it take for some of you to realize that there is no such thing as a longhaired light-skinned Nubian princess
Yes
Stolen moments created the master's child
But, dark skinned folks was sweatin' in the fields all the while
While some of your ancestors literally passed
Passed their mamas by

Denying the DNA on the inside
Now, after all the years
All the tears
Some of us have allowed ourselves to be tricked just like Malcolm said
Yes
You are being read
Frontin' like what I said ain't true
So whatcha' gonna do?
I control my own opinions
Not you

911

Someone just tried to kill me
I called 911
But, all circuits were busy

Two planes just shut down New York City
Now you're tellin' me
That all these men came from overseas
With the primary goal of bringing America to its knees
Hard to believe
We didn't check their ID's
Before they used our own machines for a killing spree

Lord, have mercy on me

LOVE, PASSION, & PAIN

Mother To Son (The First Time)

I want you to treat her tenderly.
Admire her.
Wrap your arms around her.
Shower her with kisses.
She is the most beautiful woman in the world tonight.
Make her comfortable.
Create an Eden to be shared because the two of you are there for a moment in time.
A moment you've never seen before and will never see again.
Be her nearest and dearest friend.

I want you to rub her shoulders.
Softly brush away the hair from her eyes.
Wipe her tears with your fingertips, if she cries.
Make her feel secure.
Show her with every motion, every word that you love her.
You need her.
Tell her with your eyes that she makes you complete.

I want you to experience what I felt back then.
The first time.
The time a man held me differently than before.
Touched me in a way I never felt before.
Admired my virgin body.

Made me feel secure.
The first time.
The time which created you.

Interludes

Come into my temple.
What a heavenly invitation
Extended only to the chosen one.
I yearn for the curiosity of your lips.
I desire.
I want.
I need them to probe into and between parts of me yet unseen by the common man.
I remember the last time that I experienced the intensity of your touch, being engulfed by your strength and moved by your Black beauty.

The pores of my skin thirst for the liquid of your tongue.
Daily.
I remember the last time you covered my body like glaze.
My chocolate Adonis, I find myself fascinated by the sight of your sculptured onyx body.
Perfect.

Remembering the nights, mornings, the afternoons when you anointed my body with your kisses.
You blessed me with your touch.
With each rhythmic thrust and slow grind you made me tremble with ecstasy.

It shattered the corners of my mind
Left me craving for more.

Two lovers intermingling in a dance of the body.
The soul.
As we bask in the serene glory of God given pleasure.
Seizing each moment which the universe has awarded us.
As you become part of me
And I part of you.
Waiting in anticipation of our next interlude.

Whatever

Whatever you want
I'll do it
Whatever you need
I'll get it
Wherever you go
I'll be beside you
Whenever you need me
All you have to do is call my name

If I close my eyes
I can actually feel you next to me
Having me, holding me
As I drift to sleep, you are my dreams
Thoughts of you set me free

I love the way you do what you do
All the things that make you u
I love the way you do what you do

Let me be your strength when you're weak
Your source of inspiration when you speak
Let me be the one to catch you when you fall
Be your biggest cheerleader as you give the world your all
You belong with me

Take my heart
My hopes, dreams and fears are yours to share
No one else is meant to share this space but you
Take my mind.
Make it wander
My thoughts are of you

So, do whatever
Feel whatever

Whatever you want
Whatever you need
Sweetness, its all for you

Can I?

Can I take you to a place where only lovers dwell?
Where we'll share secrets that we will never tell
Can I?

Can I have your permission to explore all the possibilities?
And see the parts of you that the world never sees

I mean…Our love has grown deeper these days
So, can I touch you in ways that no one else ever will?
And penetrate those places that in your soul that no one else could ever fill
Can I?

Can I just sit here and admire you?
'Cause there is something about your body that got me awestruck
It's got me paralyzed and though I try
I can't move my eyes

Can I whisper in your ear?
And tell you how what I need my dear.
Can I kiss you here?
Here?
And here?

ALLE

Can I taste that dark chocolate?
And eat until I just can stop it
Can I?

As you spread me like butter
You make my heart flutter
And pit-pat
As we rock from front to back
Can I tell you that you make my body sing in any other key but flat?
Damn, I dig that

Can I be your earth?
And you my sun
Can we forever be one?

Mojo

Words flow from his full-blackened lips
Like the water of the Nile
With a familiar tone
Almost similar to a Coltrane melody
Rhythmic.
Smoove.

The intensity of his eyes
Beauty of his sun-kissed skin
His soulful energy
It has all convinced me that I've found perfection personified
The pinnacle of humankind

I pinch myself to see if I'm dreaming
Yes, he is here…
In my space
In my time
Making me feel like I can fall 500 feet and survive
I can fly
I can fly…

Tomorrow, I'll build pyramids in Eqypt out of grains of sand without using my hands
Yes, I can…
If I'm powered by the love of my man

Untitled

Dead roses in a vase, an unopened bottle of wine and uneaten strawberries sit on the counter.
Reminding me of days gone by.
A love once known.

With drawn curtains, I wallow in sorrow.
Freely rolling from one side of the bed to the other in a repeated motion.
No arms, no warm body to keep me from reaching the other side.
With half-closed eyes my feet sink in puddles of water on the floor.

The body is feeling weaker than before because you broke my heart last night.
Left me staring at an empty room.
Forcing me to listen to my own echoes.
Leaving nothing but darkness, dry lips and a body untouched.

Oreo

I found out that you've living two lives
One by day, the other by night
But, which part of an Oreo do you really like?

You brought the chocolate home to meet your family
And convinced them that I was the one to carry your name and wear that three karat Tiffany ring
Then, you brought in the vanilla on our love thing

She is the opposite of me
I've got two degrees and she doesn't have a GED
I'm child-free
She's got three children that she can't feed
And . . . all her beauty must be internal
Or, do you see something that I can't see?
Must be.
But, I won't let you put her inside of me
Cause' there can only be two people in a relationship
Not three
So, I'm making the choice easy

You can have the middle

Goodbye (His Breakup Poem)

It's not you, it's me
It's just that I can't do the work to make this relationship what it should be
And when I look at the impact my actions have had on you
This is the best thing for us to do

Now, I'm not saying that you don't mean anything to me
I care for you
Thank you for being who you are
You have a good heart
But, we need to be apart

Maybe if we meet again at another time
You'll have yours and I'll have mine
Then, we can try again
Right now I need time for me
I know this is hard for you to see
I know this is difficult to understand
Cause you trusted me enough to put your heart in my hands

It hurts me to see you go
So much you'll never know
Maybe it's better for us both

So, when you walk out the door please don't turn around anymore
I don't want you to see me fall on my knees and cry
Until we meet again
Goodbye.

Double Identity

There was a time when my world revolved around you.
My first thought in the morning.
Only thought in the afternoon.
Last thought at night.

I carried your picture with me.
You occupied my senses to the highest degree.
I could not see anything but your smile.
Touch anything but your skin.
Smell only your pheromones.
Hear you call my name.

You carried my picture along with his.
My physical presence was the only thing which reminded you of my existence.
While you were touching another man's body.
Smelling a mixture of his cologne and my perfume.
Calling his name.
Tasting his sweat.
Splitting your life in two.
Keeping half of yourself in the closet.
Until I went in and turned on the lights.
Exposing your love for the missionary and the priest.

Commitments

When I look into your eyes
I see someone with the power to save my life
You should've been my wife

See, I'm Marvin's troubled man
Each day I find myself troubled by the symbol on my left hand
As we steal time like thieves
Until alarm clocks remind us of the reality once again
That another secret night must end

Baby, I stood before God and promised her
For better or worse
Richer or poorer
In sickness and in health
'Til death do us part
I simply cannot stand the fact that my actions would break her heart

I don't love her
But, I can't leave her
'Cause my word is my bond
Sometimes I wish I could wave a magic wand . . . and turn her into you
Unfortunately that's something that I can't do

So, just hold on until the day that I make my promises to you
And I'll probably break those too

For better or worse
Richer or poorer
In sickness and in health
'Til death do us part

98 You (I Understand Now)

Baby, I don't understand
Why?
Why don't you wanna be my man?
I thought that we were always gonna be together
Me for you
You for me
Got me singing "Gotta be"
Givin' me continuous ecstasy

Now, here I stand in my county browns ready to be tried in the case of heart vs. mind
My heart tells me that you are my destiny
While my mind stays closed like corporate boardrooms to Blacks
Closed like country clubs to the poor
Closed to the notion that you ain't feelin' me
No more
No more
No encores
Why are you punishing me?
Fightin' me like Ali
Keepin' me from giving you the love you need
Now, I'm blind
One day I'll see
I'll see why you and I could never be

If

If I fall for you as slowly as a leaf in November
Will you catch me?
Or, let me tumble to the ground
Guess I'll be crowned tomorrow's fool
If the latter is true
What should I do?
If seasons change
And you're not into me
Like I'm into you

Should I take your words as those made only in kind?
Or, do thoughts of me occupy the inner spaces of your mind?
If I open myself up to this opportunity
Can you promise me no games of hide and seek?
That you'll be strong for me when I'm weak
Or, have we been speaking words without substance from day to day to day?
As I sit here with a leaf in my hand
Wondering if…
If you truly want me in your life in a significant way

Afterword

I woke up this morning. Woke up and saw the rising of the sun. I've been blessed with one more day. One more day to live. Another day to see flowers in bloom. A day to try and to fail. Another day to overcome obstacles to my success. A day to take a stand. A day to make a difference. One more day to touch the life of someone else. Another day to give love and reach out for love.

Hope greeted me on my doorstep this morning. He wrapped his arms around my body and whispered in my ear. He told me to "keep on keeping on." It was at that moment that I realized that I'd finally been to the mountaintop. I'd finally become free. AMEN.

The most powerful entity in the universe is not a person
It is a word
One word can start a war
One word can bring it to an end
So, my brothers and sisters put down your guns
And pick up your pens

ALLE

JOURNAL

Let Your Inner Journey Begin

ALLE

ALLE

ALLE

ALLE

ALLE

ALLE

ALLE

ALLE

ALLE

ALLE

ALLE

ALLE

ALLE